A DAY IN THE LIFE OF AN AIRLINE PILOT

By

ROBERT LAWRENCE

Contact Information:

vegetarianpilot@gmail.com

howtobecomeanairlinepilot.org

amuchbetterlife.com

"Because every human invention and creation began with a thought, our thoughts must also create our lives."

Robert Lawrence

PREFACE

My name is Robert Lawrence. I am an airline pilot. Before I became an airline pilot, I served in the military; graduated from the University of Washington; completed one semester of law school; endured a variety of unfulfilling jobs; was employed as a flight instructor; worked in law enforcement; and otherwise lived a normal life. However, when I reached age 48, I committed to becoming an airline pilot. I made the commitment because I was thoroughly dissatisfied with my paper-shuffling desk job. I craved a life of adventure. Also, I love a challenge. Becoming an airline pilot was the biggest challenge of my life!

Before becoming an airline pilot I imagined that pilots earned huge salaries, travelled to exotic locations, and cavorted with beautiful people. I was mistaken.

I thought you might enjoy reading about the actual life of an airline pilot. In this book I explain how I prepare for a flight; what happens in the flight deck; why delays occur; and what I do when I am done flying for the day. I also share passenger behaviors that drive flight crews crazy. Enjoy the trip!

TABLE OF CONTENTS

INTRODUCTION

To begin this story, let me explain how airline crew scheduling works. Unlike most people, I do not work a 9–5 schedule, Monday thru Friday. Instead, each month I bid for the schedule I want to work the following month. Since I bid against other pilots, there is no guarantee I will be awarded my ideal schedule. The most senior pilot with my airline will always be awarded his or her desired schedule, because he or she has priority over every pilot in the company. The pilot with the least seniority will be awarded the worst schedule. Seniority is everything in the airline industry. If I was hired one hour before Joe Pilot, I will always be senior to Joe Pilot.

I can bid to fly to specific destinations; fly certain days; and work a fixed number of hours each day, week, or month. Some pilots prefer two-day trips; others prefer four-day trips. A four-day trip means I will be away from home four days. I can bid to fly 60 hours or 100 hours monthly, or anything in between. I can request to fly with crew members I like and avoid crew members I dislike. Airlines prefer that pilots avoid each other when personality conflicts exist. I enjoy a good relationship with nearly all the pilots with whom I fly. However, I currently have two pilots on my NO FLY list! Just imagine if you could avoid an irritating co-worker. You would put them on your list too!

You're probably thinking that pilots don't work as many hours as the general public. Yes, and no. I usually do not fly 40 hours or more weekly. However, as an airline pilot, I do not begin earning any pay until the aircraft main cabin door closes. That's why pilots are always in a hurry to close the damn door! Also, I stop getting paid when the main cabin door opens at the end of each flight. I am not paid when I am a passenger on the shuttle bus from the airport parking lot. I am not paid while I am waiting to pass through airport security. I am not paid while I am reviewing weather reports. I am not paid while I am inspecting the plane before we depart. I am not paid while passengers are boarding. For every two hours I work; I am only paid one hour, more or less. I bet you did not know this.

Most pilots' number one (#1) complaint is that we are underpaid. Our #2 complaint is that we fly too often. Our #3 complaint is that we are underpaid. You would think that pilots are happy in their careers. Before becoming an airline pilot, I had thought so too. However, I have since learned that pilots complain all the time. Most pilots have forgotten, or simply do not know, how bad it can be working in an office affixed to planet earth. Until

2015, I worked in an office. I was tied to my desk 9 hours daily. I still remember how much I disliked my desk job. I often stared out the window, wishing I was somewhere else. Flying airplanes is my second career, so I am grateful that I am paid to travel. I rarely complain (except about the low pay!).

Back to the schedule—like I mentioned, I became an airline pilot in 2015. In 2017, I finally acquired enough seniority to bid for a fixed work schedule. Before I had earned sufficient seniority, my employer assigned me to work a "reserve schedule." I had no choice. Reserve schedules require pilots to be "on-call." Being on-call means I must report to the airplane in as few as 2 hours, if called.

I am currently based at the Los Angeles International Airport (LAX). Before Los Angeles, I had to commute to work in Chicago, because that is where new hire pilots were needed. When I had enough seniority, I requested and was awarded LAX as my domicile. Thank goodness! I like Chicago, but it's way too cold for me there.

Reserve duty can be assigned as short, or long-call. Short-call reserve means that if I am contacted by Crew Support, I have 2 hours to report to the airplane. On long-call reserve, I have 12 hours to report to the aircraft. Since I live 60 miles north of

Los Angeles, I also rent a studio apartment near LAX, so I have somewhere to stay while on reserve duty. I pay for the apartment out of my own pocket. Crew Support could call at 6:00 a.m. and direct me to report to the aircraft for an 8:00 a.m. flight. Given the terrible traffic in Los Angeles, I could never make it to LAX within 2 hours from my home in Ventura County.

Crew Support will call if another first officer calls in sick, or the pilot originally assigned to the flight is unable to get to the airplane for some reason. On reserve, I can also be assigned to fly a trip originating from an airport other than LAX. For example, Crew Support might direct me to report to LAX within 2 hours, and then fly me as a passenger to Omaha. From Omaha, I might fly to the east coast, or I might fly passengers back to LAX. On reserve, I never know where I am flying until I am called.

Sometimes I am directed to "reposition" an empty plane. I once flew as a passenger from LAX to Boise, Idaho. I then flew an empty plane from Boise to Denver. In Denver, another crew took possession of the plane and flew it elsewhere, with passengers. I flew as a passenger back to LAX on another flight.

On reserve duty, I rarely know how long I will be away on a trip, so I always pack as if I will be away four days. The early morning reserve duty period lasts from 4 a.m. to 4 p.m. Evening reserve begins at 9:00 a.m. and ends at 9 p.m. I can be called to fly anytime during that 12-hour window.

Pilots on long-call reserve might live hundreds of miles from their domicile because they have 12 hours to report to the airplane, if called. Airline pilots fly free on most domestic carriers, provided there is an open seat in the cabin, or the extra (jump) seat in the flight deck is available.

For a variety of reasons, many pilots commute to their domicile. One reason pilots commute is because they cannot afford to purchase a home near their domicile. Many pilots with whom I fly are based at LAX, but it's too costly for them to purchase homes in Los Angeles, so they purchase homes in Arizona and commute to work in Los Angeles. That's why you often see several pilots in the back of the plane. It's because they are commuting to or from work.

Are you wondering if I still get paid if Crew Support does not call me? Yes, I still get paid, even if I do not fly the entire month. Sometimes that actually happens. While assigned to reserve duty, I am paid a minimum of 76 flight hours, even if I never leave my house. Not a bad deal. Still, pilots complain.

Now that I have enough seniority to bid for a fixed schedule, I bid to fly the first half of the month and not work the remainder of the month. I like being home with my wife and two cool cats. While I am home, I enjoy writing books; walking on the beach; sailing; hiking; and riding my motorcycle. On the contrary, I do not enjoy staying in hotels by myself and being away from home. You might be wondering why I became an airline pilot if I don't like being away from home. Because I like a challenge, that's why!

Like I mentioned earlier, when I was first hired as an airline pilot in 2015, I was based in Chicago, at O'Hare International Airport. In Chicago, I was placed on short-call reserve. Since I had no seniority, I was unable to choose my domicile or work schedule. I showed up where, and when I was told. From my home in California, I had to commute to Chicago every week and be available to fly on short notice. Because I had to report to O'Hare within 2 hours while on reserve duty, I rented a "crash pad" in Chicago.

A crash pad is a private home which is rented to flight crews from various airlines. Crash pads are furnished with bunk beds, and include a common area and kitchen. There is no privacy in a crash pad. It cost $375 monthly to stay in my Chicago crash pad.

I paid extra for a bedroom that only contained two bunk beds. This was preferable to sleeping in the basement. The basement contained 12 bunk beds and included lots of snoring and methane gas, if you know what I mean.

When I was commuting to Chicago, I only earned $36 per flight hour. Fortunately, I have a pension from a prior career, a working spouse, and a lifetime of savings and investments, so it was not a hardship for me to pay rent at a crash pad, in addition to paying a mortgage. However, for a younger pilot, who might be saddled with $125,000 in flight training debt, paying rent at a crash pad can be a financial hardship.

While based in Chicago, if my reserve duty began Saturday at 4:00 a.m., I had to try and depart LAX early Friday morning to ensure I made it to Chicago by Friday night. It was my responsibility to get to Chicago. My employer does not care where I live, they only care that I report to work on time. Sometimes I was unable to get a seat on the first two or three flights to Chicago. Remember, commuting pilots only fly free if an empty seat is available. After all, airlines are in the business of selling seats. Airlines do not earn revenue from pilots commuting to and from work, so we are low priority passengers.

I could wait several hours trying to get a seat to Chicago.

You might wonder why airlines allow pilots to fly free. It is because every airline employs pilots who live outside their domicile and commute to work. A United Airlines pilot might commute to his domicile in Dallas on Delta Airlines. A Delta Airlines pilot might commute to her New York domicile on United Airlines. Pilots look out for each other because we understand it is stressful getting to and from work. Also, pilots from competing airlines have a common bond; we all complain!

When I finally landed in Chicago, I walked 15 minutes to the train station, rode on the train for 35 minutes, and walked 10 minutes to my crash pad with my suitcase and flight bag in tow. I stayed at the Chicago crash pad four days, unless a trip was assigned. After four days on reserve, I had two days off. In those two days I had to commute home; wash my laundry; re-pack my suitcase; iron my uniform; pet my wife; kiss my cats; and fight traffic to and from LAX. Commuting is no fun. In fact, it sucks!

Chapter One

PACKING FOR A TRIP

When I return home from a four-day trip, the first thing I do is pack my suitcase for my next trip. After my clothes are laundered, I iron one uniform shirt and one pair of black slacks. I replace the epaulets, wings, and nametag on my shirt. I place a pen, earplugs, passport, and scratch paper in my shirt pocket. My uniform is then hung in the closet with my belt and company identification attached to the hangar. I am a creature of habit.

I always pack a second pilot uniform in my suitcase. I wear each uniform two days. After two days of flying, I iron my clean shirt and clean pants in my hotel room. I then wear my second uniform for the remainder of the trip. I pack an extra pilot shirt if I have a five-day trip assigned. However, since I only travel with 2 pair of pants, I simply shake out my second pair of pants on day five and hope you don't notice. Pilot life is not glamorous.

I buy a cheap suitcase every year because no matter how expensive the case, it will fall apart after one year of constant travel. My suitcase fits in the overhead bin, just like yours. In addition to packing several cans of soup and six packages of oatmeal in my suitcase, I pack three white t-shirts; three pair of black socks; three pair of underwear; walking shorts; jeans; gym shorts; a gym shirt; dressy sneakers; one black t-shirt; one shirt with a collar; a fleece jacket if it's cold where I'm travelling; one pair of ankle socks; a baseball hat; and a toiletry kit with lots of sunscreen. I was assured that the windows in the flight deck deter UV rays. However, I have my doubts, so I am always slathered in sunscreen when flying.

I also travel with a large flight bag which doubles as a lunch bag. My flight bag contains more than food. In the bag I carry my noise-cancelling pilot headset with extra batteries, and my company provided tablet computer. The tablet is loaded with electronic manuals and aviation charts. I rely on these charts for every flight. Sometimes I review the company manuals, especially if I am having trouble sleeping at night.

When I first began flying as an airline pilot in 2015, paper charts were still being used. Since pilots had to access navigation charts for nearly every commercial airport in the United States, Canada, Mexico, the Caribbean, and beyond, we carried thousands of paper charts in the flight deck. The paper charts required lots of space and had to be updated constantly. Also, they were difficult to read when flying at night. What a hassle. Thank goodness for electronic charts!

My flight bag also contains lots of "borrowed" hotel pens, notepads, a phone charger, extra ear plugs, extra eye glasses, a flashlight, and more sunscreen. Before I leave on a trip I always prepare and pack several sandwiches, yogurts, snack bars, fruit, nuts, and a frozen ice pack to keep my food cold until I get to the hotel at the end of each work day.

Before beginning a trip I ensure my tablet computer is updated and fully charged. I also review airport charts and highlight relevant information. For example, if I know I will be flying to Albuquerque the following day, I review Albuquerque charts and highlight radio frequencies. I also review charts to learn if there are unusual requirements at a particular airport. For example, some airports do not have the ability to pump cool air into the airplane, so pilots must remember to turn on the auxiliary power unit (APU) after landing, so air conditioning will continue flowing into the cabin after we arrive at the gate and shut down the engines. Before each trip I also review the airport door security codes so I can access the ramp area and visually inspect the airplane after each landing.

Once, after landing in Minneapolis in February, I exited the plane and made my way to the ramp to inspect the plane. I was not wearing my pilot jacket since I had mistakenly believed I was Superman. The aircraft inspection lasted less than three minutes. However, with the freezing temperature and fierce wind in Minneapolis that day, I began suffering the effects of hyperthermia almost immediately. Following the aircraft inspection, I climbed the stairs to the jet bridge with the intention of returning to the warm airplane. Unfortunately, I had forgotten the door code and was locked outside. No problem, I thought. I looked on my phone to obtain the door code. Surprisingly, my fingers were too numb to work the phone. I found myself unable to escape the frigid weather, while wearing only my short-sleeve pilot shirt. Not smart. I pounded on the jet bridge door, but nobody heard, or they chose to ignore the pilot; too dumb to wear a jacket in Minnesota in February. I feared I could die within minutes. Fortunately, a ramp worker eventually came to my assistance and saved my life. I learned two important lessons that day: memorize the door code and always wear a jacket in Minneapolis during the winter.

Chapter Two

DRIVING TO THE AIRPORT

As I mentioned earlier, I live about 60 miles north of the Los Angeles International Airport (LAX). LAX is my domicile, meaning all my flights originate out of LAX. When I am assigned a trip, I have to arrive at the aircraft at least 35 minutes prior to the scheduled departure time. Because of vehicle traffic congestion in Los Angeles, I give myself three hours to get to the airport. I never want to keep you waiting. Plus, I suffer from obsessive compulsive disorder (OCD), so I arrive everywhere early. I will probably be the first one to arrive at my funeral.

I have a key card which opens a gate at the employee parking lot. The lot is located approximately one mile from LAX, directly under the flight path of runway 24 right. After parking, I clip on my neck tie, remove my suitcase and flight bag from my trunk, and walk to the shuttle bus stop. I sometimes wait 30 minutes for a bus to arrive. I could complain about this for two chapters but will save my complaint for another book. Often, the bus is so crowded there is standing room only. Flight crews, TSA workers, rampers, gate agents, and others pack into the shuttle bus like sardines. The bus crawls along in heavy traffic, often taking 30 minutes to arrive at the departure terminal. Yesterday, the bus broke down and I walked the last ¼ mile to the terminal.

When I exit the shuttle, it's always a chaotic scene at LAX. There are hundreds, maybe thousands of passengers on the sidewalk waiting for their friends; family; shuttle vans; limousines; or Uber. Most people appear unaware that sidewalks and corridors should be treated as roadways. Meaning, pedestrians should keep to their right when walking, just like we keep to our right when driving. We never stop our car in the middle of the road; so don't stand in the middle of the sidewalk. Keep to your right and don't block sidewalks and corridors!

As an airline pilot, I am able to bypass regular TSA security screening. I enter the airport via a Known Crew Member (KCM) checkpoint. KCM is available to flight crews at most large airports in the United States. At the KCM checkpoint, I present my airline identification, KCM badge, and passport. If I was unable to bypass regular TSA screening, I would quit working as an airline pilot and pursue employment elsewhere. I could write about the TSA for two chapters, but you already know what I have to say about the TSA, so I will leave it unsaid.

Once past airport security, I check in for my flight using my mobile phone. Once checked in, my employer and flight crew are alerted that I am in the airport and past security. If I fail to check in at least 35 minutes prior to the scheduled departure time, Crew Support will call. If I do not answer my phone, Crew Support will contact a reserve pilot and direct him or her to report to the aircraft. Fortunately, this has never happened to me. I am always early and have never missed a flight.

Chapter Three

INSIDE THE AIRPORT

Once past airport security, I make my way to my company crew lounge. At LAX, the employee lounge is located under a passenger terminal. The crew lounge is noisy and resembles a dungeon, because it lacks natural light. The lounge contains a few pieces of furniture; several computers; a printer and copy machine; microwave and sink; and metal racks to store luggage. There is also a "quiet room" nearby which is a little less noisy than the crew lounge. The quiet room is furnished with several leather recliners so pilots and flight attendants can rest or sleep between flights. Who knows what else is going on in there!

Inside the crew lounge, pilots and flight attendants print trip sheets and complain to each other about the low pay and long work days. A trip sheet lists each leg of an assigned work block. For example, if I am scheduled to fly a four-day trip, I might fly 3 legs the first day, and 4 legs the next day, and so on. A leg equals one takeoff and landing. A flight from LAX to Denver is considered one leg. A trip sheet includes the flight number, as well as the names of each crew member assigned to the trip. The trip sheet also includes hotel information, so I know where I will be staying at the end of each work day.

In addition to trip sheets, pilots print flight releases in the crew lounge. The flight release is available one hour before our scheduled departure time. A flight release contains the following information: the flight number; planned altitude; fuel required; crew names; expected flight time; weather at the departure and arrival airports; expected turbulence; taxiway and runway closures; airport lighting outages; and a host of other relevant information. If you see a pilot at the departure gate and he or she is flipping through several pages of paper, the pilot is probably reviewing the flight release. Or, maybe they were just served with divorce papers. I have no idea.

Flight releases are prepared by airline dispatchers. If pilots have concerns about the upcoming flight, we can call the dispatcher for clarification. I have never met a dispatcher in person and suspect they might actually be robots.

Chapter Four

ACCESSING THE PLANE

I sometimes meet my fellow crew members for the first time when I arrive at the aircraft at the beginning of a trip. I usually fly with the same crew during the entire trip. However, sometimes a pilot or flight attendant will fly only part of a trip, then a different pilot or flight attendant will work the remainder of the trip.

My airline employs more than 4,000 pilots and an equal or greater number of flight attendants, so I am always meeting new people. Sometimes flight crews get to know each other, and other times we remain strangers. I recently flew with a captain who only spoke to me when I read the checklist. Talk about a weirdo. He was a great pilot but he has been added to my NO FLY LIST.

I check-in with the gate agent once my plane has arrived. It's important to coordinate with the gate agent so he or she knows that the outbound flight crew has arrived. Gate agents verify the crews' identification and grant access to the plane via the jet bridge. Gate agents are always in a hurry to begin boarding because when they are done working our flight; they have to prepare for other flights.

In my opinion, gate agents have the most difficult job in all of aviation. Last year, while waiting at a departure gate in Chicago, I witnessed a passenger drop to the floor while screaming like a spoiled child. The passenger thrashed about on the floor while ranting hysterically because she had been told that her suitcase was too large to fit in the overheard bin, and would have to be checked. The gate agent remained calm and professional during the spectacle. I don't have patience for this type of nonsense. I prefer being locked behind the flight deck door. Some of you in the back are out-of-your mind!

When a plane parks at the gate, the outbound crew meets the inbound crew in the jet bridge and shares relevant information. Usually, the inbound crew just wants to get the hell out of there and go home or get to their hotel. I know the feeling. The inbound crew is responsible to contact maintenance if there are any mechanical concerns. Mechanics usually respond within minutes to resolve any issues. However, not every airport has mechanics available. If no mechanics are stationed at an airport, the mechanics must drive, or be flown in to resolve mechanical issues. For example, I once landed in Ontario, California, and the plane was grounded because of a mechanical issue. No, it wasn't my fault. My airline does not have a maintenance base at Ontario, so mechanics drove to Ontario from Palm Springs. The drive took several hours due to heavy traffic, of course. Upon arrival, mechanics resolved the maintenance issue within minutes, but the flight crew and passengers were delayed several hours. Not that you care, but I was not paid during the delay.

When our airplane is taken out-of-service for a mechanical issue, schedulers (also robots) arrange for a replacement aircraft. When mechanics have resolved the maintenance issue, the repaired plane is returned to service and replaces the plane that was "borrowed."

There are so many variables in aviation it is a miracle that flights operate as smoothly as they do. There are literally hundreds of things that can go wrong every day. Bad weather a thousand miles away can affect your flight. A flat tire a thousand miles away can affect your flight. A sick pilot a thousand miles away can affect your flight. A computer outage can affect your flight. An unruly passenger can affect your flight. You get the picture. When delays happen, for whatever reason, the pilots, mechanics, flight attendants, gate agents, schedulers, ATC, rampers and others work together to resolve issues as quickly as possible. Trust me, we are always doing our best to get you to your destination on time. We want to get there too.

As I enter the plane for the first time, I verify the aircraft registration matches the registration number on the flight release. The aircraft I fly all look alike. In fact, I might fly three different planes in one day. I have heard stories of pilots flying the wrong airplane to their destination. You as a passenger would never know, but the FAA would be notified and the pilots would have some explaining to do.

When I enter the flight deck I ensure the required safety equipment is present. I verify that I have a life vest behind my seat, a flashlight near my right leg, and an escape rope above my head. There is also a crash ax, fire extinguisher, and a personal breathing device (PBD) in the flight deck. By the way, I can't get my cuticle scissors through airport security but I have an ax in the flight deck. Oh yeah, I also fly the plane! Wait, I said I wasn't going to say anything about the TSA. Anyway, the PBD allows one of the pilots to see the flight controls and have access to breathable air if smoke ever fills the flight deck. In the flight deck I also ensure the circuit breaker are set correctly and then I build my nest. Building my nest means I position my seat to the correct height; move the rudder pedals a comfortable distance from my seat; plug in my headset; and affix my tablet computer to a bracket near my right leg. I also attach scratch paper to a nearby writing surface so I can copy taxi instructions and clearances.

I utilize a checklist to establish power if the plane is "dark" when I arrive. In aviation, nearly everything involves a checklist. The Safety & Power Up Checklist allows pilots to confirm that the appropriate switches, levers, and buttons are in the correct position before applying power, or starting the auxiliary power unit (APU). The APU is a mini-jet engine housed in the tail of the plane. The APU provides air conditioning (air pressure) and electrical power. You will know if the APU is operating because you can hear it when you board the plane.

Usually, while the aircraft is parked at the gate, the plane is actually plugged in like a big toaster. If you look out the terminal window before you board you might notice a thick cord hanging from the nose of the airplane. That is a power cord. A ramper plugs the power cord into the plane when we arrive at the gate. The cord is unplugged after we start the APU, or prior to pushing away from the gate.

Once power has been established, I initialize the flight computer by inputting my password. I also review the airplane maintenance log to ensure mechanics have resolved any recent issues and signed the logbook to confirm the plane is airworthy. Once I have completed these tasks, I exit the airplane via the jet bridge and perform an exterior inspection of the plane. During my inspection, I look for damage, such as a bird strike. I ensure there are no fluid leaks; the antennas and probes are present; navigation lights are working properly; landing gear is in good condition; and there is sufficient tread on the tires, etc. The aircraft I fly are well built and the maintenance crews are truly amazing, so it is rare to find any problems during my visual inspection.

When you are seated inside the terminal you might see a pilot walking around the plane. He or she is performing an inspection. The first officer performs the inspection 99% of the time. If you see the pilot taking a "selfie" next to the plane it's probably me. I am still trying to get the right cover photo for this book. So far every picture I have taken makes me look like an idiot. Wait, maybe the Minneapolis incident means....

The below photo was taken during an exterior inspection in Seattle.

Following the inspection, I return to the plane. Once all crew members are present, the captain conducts an ICE briefing before passengers begin boarding. The "I" in ICE briefing refers to introductions. I forget what C & E refer to. I hope C & E aren't important. Anyway, a crew briefing is conducted at the beginning of a trip. During the briefing, the captain reviews security protocols; flight time; expected turbulence; any inoperative equipment; and what we can expect should an emergency arise. Following the briefing I continue programming the flight computer. I enter our expected departure route; anticipated departure runway; speed limits (if any); fuel reserves; and other relevant information. The official name for the flight computer is actually the flight management system (FMS). Pilots call the FMS "the box," because it takes too long to say "flight management system."

While passengers are boarding, I request the latest airport weather report. At the top of each hour, a new weather report is recorded and made available at most airports. The weather report is known as an ATIS. ATIS is an acronym for "automated terminal information service." The ATIS is a continual broadcast of aeronautical information, generally related to local weather and airport conditions. I can obtain the ATIS via "the box" and print the ATIS using the onboard printer. However, at smaller airports, such as Colorado Springs, I must listen to the ATIS broadcast on the radio. Each ATIS broadcast includes a phonetic letter identifier, such as Alpha (A), Bravo (B), or Charlie (C), etc. I have to provide the phonetic identifier to the ground controller, prior to taxi, and to the approach controller during our arrival. By providing the identifier, I alert the controller that I have listened to the most recent ATIS report. If weather conditions change significantly within the hour, a new ATIS is generated and a new phonetic identifier is also provided.

Once I have programmed the flight management system (FMS), I perform an originating flow. A flow is a memorized scan and/or hand movement to verify switch positions, etc. During the flow, I verify that my primary flight display (PFD) is functioning properly, the heading bug is selected for the expected departure runway, the altimeter is set correctly, and the source selector is pointed toward the flying pilot. The PFD is essentially a computer monitor. The monitor is positioned directly in front of me. The captain has a separate PFD. The PFD provides a variety of critical information during flight; such as bank angle; climb or descent rate; airspeed, and heading information etc.

The primary flight display is depicted below on the right. The multi-function display is pictured on the left. On the PFD you can see the ground speed is 434 knots (500 miles per hour). The altitude is 25,120', climbing to 36,000', on a heading of 317 degrees.

During my "flow" I also verify that my oxygen mask is functioning and the emergency landing gear extension handle is secure. When both the captain and I have completed our respective originating flows, the captain requests the originating checklist be read. The captain requests every checklist, except the descent checklist. The pilot flying always calls for the descent checklist. I should point out that the captain and first officer take turns flying. Many people wrongly believe that only the captain flies the plane. Not true. Sometimes the captain and first officer fly every other leg, and sometimes we fly two legs before switching roles. If I am not the pilot flying (PF), I am the pilot monitoring (PM). The pilot monitoring is responsible for all radio calls and mentally flies the airplane without actually touching the controls. The captain and I always back each other up. That's why there are two pilots in the flight deck. If I miss something, the captain will point it out, and vice versa.

When the captain calls for the originating checklist, I grab the checklist from the console and read the checklist, as written. For example, I might read, "Gear pins," and the captain would respond, "Removed." I would then verify that the gear pins had been removed by also responding, "Removed." I know the gear pins have been removed because I looked for them during the exterior aircraft inspection. When a checklist is read, each pilot verifies that the item has been completed. Once the originating checklist is complete, I say, "Originating checklist complete."

Thirty minutes prior to our scheduled departure, a pre-departure clearance (PDC) becomes available.

The PDC is delivered via the onboard flight computer. I print the PDC and display it where it is visible to both pilots. The PDC lists the routing we will fly after takeoff; initial altitude; 4-digit transponder code to identify our airplane to air traffic control (ATC); and departure radio frequency. The PDC is the official clearance. After I enter the clearance information into the flight computer, both pilots verify its accuracy.

After both pilots have verified the routing, reviewed the airport taxi diagram, and obtained the latest weather, the pilot flying provides a WANT briefing to the pilot monitoring. The WANT briefing discusses the following information: W = weather; A = airport; N = notams; and T = threats.

The pilot flying always begins his or her brief WANT briefing by discussing current weather (W) conditions, using information obtained from the ATIS and flight release. If applicable, the pilot flying discusses wind shear, runway conditions, visibility, atmospheric conditions, and air temperature. If a runway is wet or covered in snow, pilots make adjustments to the flight management system. If wind shear is mentioned in the weather report, we depart with maximum thrust. We often depart with reduced thrust, to prolong engine life. Also, if it's below 10 degrees Celsius, and there is visible moisture (clouds or rain etc.), we activate the anti-icing system while still on the ground.

The pilot flying next discusses the airport (A) environment. Both pilots use their tablet computers to review the taxi route to the departure runway. At large airports, we might taxi for 10 minutes, using a variety of taxiways. Some runways are more than two miles long, so it can take several minutes to taxi to the departure runway. Sometimes we arrive at the runway and discover the wind has shifted, so we have to taxi to the other end of the runway. We prefer to takeoff into the wind, if possible.

Even at LAX, my home base, I always brief the taxi route and copy taxi instructions onto my notepad. The captain is unable to copy taxi instructions because he or she is busy "driving" the plane. The captain drives because the steering wheel is located on the left side of the flight deck, just like in a car (unless you're in England). By the way, I say "flight deck" because it is no longer politically correct to say "cock pit." Flight attendants are no longer called stewardesses because—well, I am unsure. A male flight attendant used to be called a steward, so I am unsure what was offensive about the term stewardess.

The flying pilot will also discuss "hot spots." Hot spots are locations on the ground where several taxiways and/or runways converge. Recently, an experienced pilot with my airline taxied onto the wrong taxiway in San Francisco. The taxiway is identified as a hot spot on our taxi diagram charts. The taxiway has since been permanently closed because so many other pilots have made the same mistake. Pilots are not (yet) robots and we sometimes turn left instead of right. At night, in poor visibility, at a busy airport, the most difficult part of the trip is sometimes the taxi to the departure runway. Really.

I often start the second engine during our taxi to the departure runway. The first officer always starts the engines. If I have to start the second engine during the taxi, I must focus on the airplane gauges, instead of looking outside. Starting an engine while taxiing is a threat, as it takes one minute to start each engine. The airplane only requires one engine to taxi and delaying the second engine start means we burn less fuel. Pilots prefer to land with lots of extra fuel and airlines like to save money by burning less fuel. Therefore, even though it is a threat, we often delay starting both engines until we are near the departure runway.

Let's continue the WANT briefing. After airport environment (A), the pilot flying discusses notams (N). A notam is an acronym for "notice to airmen." Airmen is the antiquated term for pilots, and applies to both male and female pilots. Notams are listed on the flight release and sometimes within the ATIS report. Notams might include runway and taxiway closures, navigation equipment outages, tall cranes nearby, and bird activity in the area. I have never understood why we brief bird activity because birds are a threat I am unable to control. I cannot swerve in flight to avoid birds because we are travelling too fast, and I would only be guessing that the birds would swerve left instead of right. On occasion, we do strike birds during takeoff or landing. I become aware of a bird strike when I observe a blood stain during my exterior inspection. All bird strikes are reported to the maintenance department. I have only observed two blood stains in 2 years.

Finally, the last item briefed is threats (T). Just so you know, pilots attempt to complete every task in an identical manner, while on the ground or in the air. However, situations always arise which create a deviation from the norm. Deviations from the norm are considered threats. We verbally identify potential threats so both pilots are aware of the threat. Threats occur on the ground as often as they occur in the air. Poor visibility is a threat. Radio and ground congestion is a threat. Weather can be a threat. Fatigue is a threat. Last minute runway changes are a threat. Feeling rushed is a threat. Personality conflict in the flight deck is a threat. Inoperative equipment is a threat. We are faced with a variety of threats during each phase of flight. Pilots attempt to mitigate each threat before it manifests into a genuine problem. You as a passenger will be unaware of most potential threats. By the way, light to moderate turbulence is generally not a threat, unless you are out of your seat or your seat belt is not fastened. I know passengers don't like bumpy rides and I don't either. However, when we encounter light to moderate turbulence we slow to a speed which prevents structural damage to the aircraft. Turbulence is a nuisance, not a threat, provided you keep your seat belt fastened. We frequently climb or descend to avoid or escape turbulence. Pilots and ATC work together to find smooth air. If we are experiencing a bumpy ride at 34,000', we will climb to 36,000', or descend to 32,000'. ATC will ask nearby flights about "their ride" in an attempt to find smooth air. Sometimes there is no smooth air. When that's the case, I just tighten my seatbelt and we turn on the seatbelt sign.

Back to the briefing. Another example of a threat can be unfamiliarity with the airplane. For instance, prior to becoming "type-rated" to fly my current jet, I flew an entirely different airplane, made in a different country. Pilots only fly one version of an airplane at a time. Why, you ask? Because switch positions; levers; and knobs in a Boeing are different than an Airbus, or Embraer, etc. The flight deck layout in a Boeing 737 is very different than the flight deck found in an Embraer 175. Think of it like this: When you first get into a rental car, it might take you a moment to identify the seat adjustment lever, trunk latch, and emergency brake release, because the configuration of the rental car varies from your personal car. In this regard, airplanes are similar to cars.

A pilot will never fly a 737 one day, then fly a 747 the following day. Pilots must know the position of every knob, switch, lever, and flap settings of the planes that we fly. Therefore, we only fly one make and model airplane at a time. When a pilot becomes certified to fly a different aircraft, the pilot must earn a "type-rating," in the new plane. Obtaining a new type-rating can take several weeks, or longer. I have earned nearly every pilot certificate available, and have also earned two separate type-ratings. Now that I am flying a bigger plane, I no longer fly the smaller plane I flew in 2016.

I have never flown a Boeing 747, nor have I ever been in the flight deck of a 747. However, if my life depended on it, and I was a passenger and the only surviving pilot onboard, I am confident I could successfully land a 747. However, I would need air traffic control to position me on a long, straight in approach to an airport with great visibility. Before landing, I would need time to figure out where the flap and gear levers are located. Forget about using the auto-pilot, as I am unsure how to operate the auto-pilot on a 747. Also, I would not know how to select or even determine the landing speeds on a 747. I would definitely need to fly to an airport with a very long runway. We would all (probably) survive, but the landing might be firm. Sorry to scare you. This is why we only fly one make and model of airplane at a time. Each version of an airplane is unique.

Like I was saying, when I transitioned to my current jet I considered myself to be a threat because I was new to the airplane. I trained two months in my current plane before I earned a type-rating and was authorized to fly a regular schedule. I studied approximately one hundred hours on my own, attended ground school for several weeks, and trained in a flight simulator for dozens of hours. I then flew with an instructor pilot in the actual plane, with passengers, before I was approved to fly my regular schedule. Keep in mind that I have been flying airplanes for nearly 20 years. However, it still takes lots of time, study, and practice to become proficient flying a new airplane.

You should take comfort in knowing that the training requirements to become an airline pilot are very demanding. When you fly you will have two highly trained and competent pilots at the controls. It is difficult to earn an Airline Transport License (ATP). An ATP license is required to fly for an airline. Despite my experience, I still considered myself to be a threat when I first transitioned to a new airplane. To mitigate this threat, airlines pair experienced captains or first officers with less experienced captains or first officers. For example, Crew Scheduling might pair a first officer with 3 years experience in a particular plane with a captain who has been flying for 10 years, but is new to a particular airplane.

Just a side note for those of you who have a fear of flying. It is odd that people who fear flying will drive on a two-lane highway, with oncoming traffic only a few feet away. Talk about terrifying! Nonetheless, people drive under these dangerous conditions every day. We have no idea if other drivers are intoxicated, texting, or tired. Despite the irony, some passengers hold tightly to their irrational fear of flying, while never expressing a similar fear of driving. Think about that.

Only the best pilots are able to become airline pilots. Earning an Airline Transport License is comparable to earning a Master's Degree, or even a PhD. Furthermore, the government regulates every aspect of airline safety, and the airlines themselves work hard to protect their passengers and reputations. Airline crashes are so rare that it is huge news when there is an actual mishap. Relax and enjoy the trip.

During a typical WANT briefing, if I am the pilot flying I might say the following during my briefing, "It's a beautiful day in Los Angeles. Winds are right down the runway at 5 knots, the ceiling (cloud layer) is broken at 2,000', it's 16 degrees Celsius and traffic is departing on runways 25 right and 24 left. I expect we will depart on runway 25 right and taxi via taxiway Bravo. Runway 25 right is 12,091 feet in length. If we lose an engine after V1, we will fly the runway heading to our clearance altitude limit of 5,000'. We can diagnose the problem in the air and return to land on runway 25 left, as runway 25 left is the longest runway available. We are assigned to fly the Casta 7 departure. We cannot exceed 250 knots on the departure. I have programmed 250 knots in the "box" and verified the departure fixes (waypoints). There are no notams that will affect our short taxi or departure. There is a lot of congestion on the ground. To mitigate that threat, I will keep my head up and copy all taxi instructions. That's my brief." The captain will discuss taxiing on one or two engines and review what to expect if we reject the take-off. Once the briefing is completed, the captain requests the before start checklist. I read the checklist and both pilots confirm the items on the checklist have been performed.

Chapter Five

PASSENGER BOARDING

Prior to passengers boarding the aircraft, flight attendants prepare the cabin. Admittedly, I have no idea what flight attendants do during this time. By the way, flight attendants complain more than pilots. While flight attendants prepare the cabin, ground personnel known as "rampers," load baggage in the forward and aft cargo bays. Also, a "fueler" pumps jet fuel into the wing tanks. The fuel load is determined by the flight dispatcher. Besides being a robot, the dispatcher is an airline employee who reviews weather reports, airport delays, and other information to determine how much fuel a flight will require. The dispatcher also selects a cruising altitude and alternate airport, just in case we are unable to land at our destination airport. Captains like to carry extra fuel, so I often direct the fueler to add 500 additional pounds of fuel. We request fuel by weight, not gallons. The airplanes I fly carry more than 20,000 pounds of fuel, or the equivalent of 3,000 gallons.

Other airport employees drain lavatory waste, add potable water, and cater the plane with meals, snacks, and beverages. Flight crews never drink the coffee made on the plane. You can, if you want. I wouldn't! Sometimes a cleaning crew shows up between flights. Other times the flight crew is responsible for cleaning the cabin. Here comes another rant: Some passengers should not be allowed to fly, let alone leave their house.

Some passengers leave dirty diapers in seat back pockets. Some passengers remove their shoes and clip their toenails on the plane. Many passengers fly in clothing unworthy of bus travel in the third world. Some passengers fly with sleeveless shirts, exposing their seat mates to their smelly armpits. Some passengers make a total mess of airplane lavatories.

My goodness! If you recognize yourself in the above paragraph, please correct your behavior or stop flying and travel by bus where you will be more comfortable. What kind of person leaves a dirty diaper in the seat pocket? Also, please end your telephone conversation before boarding the plane. It's rude to hold a conversation when others are nearby and unable to escape your verbal assault. Send a text instead. Whew!

At some point, a gate agent comes to the plane and asks if we are ready to board passengers. Welcome aboard.

Once baggage is loaded, a ramper delivers a cargo load report (CLR) to the flight deck. The CLR indicates the types of bags and their location. A carry-on bag is considered to weigh 30 pounds, regardless of its actual weight. A heavy bag is considered to weigh 60 pounds, regardless of its actual weight, unless it weighs in excess of 100 pounds, then it's actually weighed. Go figure! If pets are loaded in the cargo bay, both pilots ensure the animals are placed in the forward bay, as pets are prohibited from the aft cargo bay. I am an animal lover (and vegetarian) so I take great care to ensure your pets arrive safely, just as I would want my pets to arrive safely.

I know I just ranted but we have time for another rant. I'll be quick. The number of passengers bringing their "companion" animals on the plane is out-of-control at this point. I know you don't need a companion animal to travel with you! I cannot wait until a passenger brings their companion python and sits next to a passenger with their companion poodle.

My mom has a 200 lb. pet pig. Really. The pig is named Bob. Bob believes he is a dog. Would you mind if Bob was seated next to you? After all, Bob brings my mother comfort when she travels. Where do we draw the line? End of rant. Thank you for indulging me.

As the first officer, it is my job to enter the baggage totals into the flight computer. Actually, I always say the job of the first officer is to make the captain's life easier. Soon after I have entered baggage information into the FMS, the forward flight attendant brings a Passenger Index Number (PIN) card to the flight deck. The PIN card lists the number of passengers and their locations in each section of the cabin. The PIN card identifies passengers as adults, children, infants, and persons who will require wheel chairs upon our arrival. I enter the information into the FMS, just as I entered the baggage information. For flight planning purposes, an adult passenger weighs 190 pounds during the summer, and a child weighs 82 pounds in the summer. Adult and child weights are increased 5 pounds in the winter, presumably because of heavier clothing. Service animals are considered to be weightless (even Bob). After I have entered the passengers, baggage, and cargo totals into the FMS, the data is sent to outer space where it is mysteriously calculated and returned within seconds as performance data. The FMS provides pilots with optimal take off speeds, flaps settings, and the appropriate thrust required for departure. The FMS also alerts pilots if the plane is not balanced properly. If we are imbalanced, we move bags or move passengers. This is why we sometimes ask people in the front of the airplane to move to the back. This rarely happens on larger airplanes like the plane I am currently flying. However, weight and balance issues can affect smaller aircraft. Remember, when you remove the seats, interior paneling, and carpet, we are left with a "winged tube." It's amazing when you think about it. If we have to move a few people to the back of the tube to ensure it is balanced properly, please understand that it's done for a reason. We want the tube to be balanced so we can launch it 39,000' into the sky and bring it down safely, thousands of miles away. When the pilots make an announcement and say, "We are just finishing up some last minute paperwork," we are probably referring to the passenger and baggage paperwork, or we need time to finish a sandwich.

When the FMS returns the aircraft performance information, I read aloud the data and the captain manually inputs the information into the FMS. We both verify its accuracy. Soon thereafter, the forward flight attendant asks if it is o.k. to close the main cabin door. The captain authorizes the flight attendant to secure the main cabin door if our performance numbers are within tolerance. A gate agent then drives the jet bridge away from the airplane. Just a quick note. We sometimes get delayed at this time because late arriving bags are loaded into the cargo bay at the last moment. When this happens, we have to resubmit all the data, re-send it to outer space, and re-enter the performance data in the FMS. I know you want your luggage on the plane so we accept this delay. I only mention this to remind you, "It's never the fault of the pilots!"

Once the main cabin door is closed, an electronic message is sent to company headquarters and I finally begin receiving my hourly wage. That's why pilots are always in a hurry to close the damn door! Soon thereafter, the flight attendant returns to the flight deck and says she or he is ready for taxi. Only then is the door separating the pilots from the passengers closed and locked. Just so you know, if you want your son or daughter to come to the flight deck to say, "hi" and take a picture, please ask. I enjoy talking with kids who might be on vacation, or travelling on an airplane for the first time. Just ask the flight attendant if it's o.k. and the flight attendant will ask the pilots. If we have time we always oblige. It's probably better to visit the flight deck after we have landed.

Once the flight deck door is secure we begin gossiping about the flight attendants and eventually the captain calls for the "before start checklist." Before reading the checklist, I perform my associated "flow." My flow includes turning on the aircraft beacon so ground personnel know we are nearly ready for push back and engine start. I also turn on a hydraulic pump, verify all aircraft doors and windows are closed, and turn on the aircraft transponder so air traffic control is alerted to our location. I then read the checklist.

Chapter Six

PUSH BACK

After the before start checklist has been completed, the captain communicates with a ramper who is awaiting his or her call. The ramper wears a headset which is plugged into the nose of the aircraft. If the ramper is ready for the push, I call the Ramp Tower controller and request permission to push away from the gate. This is often where we experience a delay, because aircraft located behind our plane may be blocking our path. At LAX, we push away from the gate into an area known as the "alley." The alley is the ramp area between terminals. The alley at LAX is too narrow to accommodate more than two or three planes at a time. Therefore, aircraft from opposing terminals compete to push away from their gates, and we are frequently delayed until the alley is clear. Inbound aircraft may also be delayed from entering the alley to unload passengers, because departing aircraft are blocking the entrance. At LAX and elsewhere, I have waited up to 30 minutes before receiving permission to push away from the gate. I know passengers are frustrated during these delays, but please remember, it's never the fault of the pilots! Some of the largest airports in the country were built decades ago and are unable to accommodate the congestion we have today. Fortunately, modern airports like Denver International in Colorado are designed so that congestion is kept to a minimum when it's time to push away from the gate.

To push the plane away from the gate, a ramper connects a vehicle to the front landing gear. The vehicle is referred to as a tug. The tug pushes the airplane to a safe location where I can start the engines. After starting an engine, we can maneuver under our own power. If pilots had to back the airplane away from the gate without the use of a tug, we would have to start the engines at the gate (terminal) and use thrust reversers. We are prohibited from doing this for a variety of dangerous reasons, one of them being that we cannot see behind the airplane. Also, it would be very dangerous to start the engines at the gate. Ground personnel could be sucked into the engines and killed. Also, the reverse thrust required to move the airplane backwards would be similar to Hurricane Harvey. That's why we rely on a tug to push the airplane back from the gate.

When the Ramp Tower controller gives us clearance to push, the ramper drives the airplane backwards. Sometimes it's a smooth push, other times you might feel the plane jerk to and fro. During the pushback, I extend the flaps for takeoff. I do not extend the flaps sooner because I do not want to injure a person who might be standing next to a wing. At some point, the rampers indicate that it is safe to start our engines. The captain then says, "Start engine #1." I respond, "Starting engine #1." I lift a protective cover and turn the engine start knob while simultaneously starting a timer. I only start one engine at a time. The air conditioning "packs" close when I start an engine. As a passenger you might notice that air stops blowing from your overhead vent (gasper) during pushback. This is because the air flow created by the auxiliary power unit (APU) is diverted from the gaspers so it can be used to spin the turbine in the engine. While the engine is spooling up, my only job is to observe the instrument gauges to ensure the engine starts properly, meaning it does not overheat and/or catch fire. Yes, it happens. I have never had a problem starting an engine. Once the engine has successfully started, air begins flowing back into the cabin. After engine start, the APU is turned off because the engine is now providing electricity and air circulation.

Another reason for a delay at this time might be congestion at our destination airport. Sometimes, when I fly to San Francisco (SFO), there are too many flights trying to land, so SFO restricts the number of flights they will accept. Also, poor weather at SFO can result in fewer planes landing. When congestion or weather delays occur, a "flow" restriction is put into effect. The delay can affect flights all over the planet. If we are already in the air, en-route to San Francisco, ATC may instruct us to fly slower, so we do not arrive at SFO early and then have to circle above the airport for an hour. We may not have sufficient fuel to circle the airport for an hour, so by flying slower we burn less fuel and create a landing "window." A flow restriction may delay our flight 5 minutes, or it may delay our flight several hours. We usually do not learn of a flow restriction until we push away from the gate and contact ATC. I know passengers hate delays. I hate delays too. However, I prefer a delay when the main cabin door is closed, because when the door is closed I get paid! If the delay is too long, we will return to the gate so passengers can deplane. However, sometimes there is no gate available, so the ground controller will direct us to a location where we can park without blocking other aircraft. When we park for a delay, we usually turn on the auxiliary power unit (APU) and shut down the engines.

Chapter Seven

READY TO TAXI

After we have pushed away from the gate, started at least one engine, and completed the "After Start Checklist," I call the Ramp Tower a second time and advise that we are ready for further taxi. The ramp controller will direct our aircraft to move to a specific location, normally identified by a number painted on the concrete, and denoted on our taxi chart. Of note, different controllers are responsible for various areas of the airport.

Often, there is a lot of congestion on the radio (too many people talking at once), there may be poor visibility, and sometimes it is difficult to see taxi signs and runway markings. I am comfortable taxiing at LAX, because it is my home base. I am not nearly as comfortable taxiing at O'Hare airport in Chicago, simply because I do not fly to Chicago very often. In my opinion, taxiing at O'Hare should be offered as a college course with a PhD awarded. Yes, the hardest part of flying into O'Hare is not landing; it is maneuvering to and from the gate. Don't believe me? Type "O'Hare ground control" into YouTube and listen. Caution, your head might explode.

Before leaving the ramp area (the ramp is where airplanes park), I contact ground control and request permission to enter the taxiway. I often have to wait several minutes to contact the ground controller because there is too much congestion on the radio. Many airports have only one ground control frequency for the entire airport, so every airplane taxiing, or requesting to taxi, communicates on the same frequency.

I call the ground controller when there is split second pause on the radio. Often times, two or three pilots call simultaneously and block each other's call. It can be frustrating. When I am able to force my way in, I tell the controller who I am, where I am, and what I want. Meaning, during the initial call I provide my call sign and flight number; location at the airport; and indicate I am ready to taxi. I also provide the phonetic ATIS identifier I received with the weather report. If I do not provide the phonetic identifier, such as Zulu, the ground controller will assume I have not listened to the ATIS. My call to the ground controller might sound like this: "Los Angeles ground, Acme Airlines #4762, top of the alley Charlie 6, ready taxi with Zulu." The ground controller will respond, "Acme #4762, expect runway 25 right, taxi via Bravo, give way to company traffic, hold short Charlie 4." I repeat the taxi instructions and copy them on my note pad using short-hand. I am often unaware of our runway assignment until speaking with the ground controller. At LAX, we sometimes depart from a runway on the south side of the airport, and other times we depart from the north side.

Before we move the airplane forward, the captain asks if I am ready for taxi. If I am ready I reach up and turn on our taxi light. The taxi light is illuminated so airport vehicles, ground personnel, and other aircraft know our plane is underway. Planes always have the right-of-way over airport vehicles.

During the taxi, both the captain and I have our airport taxi diagrams visible on our respective tablet computers. If we expect to arrive at our departure runway within just a few minutes, the captain will direct me to start engine #2. I will say, "Starting engine #2." I advance the thrust lever on engine #1 so I have sufficient airflow to spin the turbine in engine #2. I then repeat the process I used to start engine #1. It usually takes one minute to start an engine. Starting an engine while taxiing is considered a threat. When I was a brand new airline pilot, I felt overwhelmed when I had to start an engine while taxiing. I would forget to advance the thrust lever on the operating engine, I failed to respond to radio calls because I was totally focused on the engine gauges, and I was sometimes unsure of our location on the ground because I was too focused on the engine gauges, instead of looking outside. Now I can start an engine in my sleep.

The photo below was taken at San Francisco while waiting for takeoff.

Chapter Eight

TAKEOFF

As the airplane nears the departure end of the runway, I monitor the tower frequency. When it appears that our plane will depart within two minutes, the captain calls for the 'Before Takeoff Checklist.' I then make an announcement to the passengers and say, "Ladies and gentlemen, we are #3 for departure. Flight attendants please be seated." I call the flight attendants to confirm the passengers are seated. You will hear a "ding" in the cabin when I call the flight attendants. After the flight attendants respond that the cabin is secure, I verify that the wheel brakes are not overheated by looking at my multi-function display screen. If we attempt to depart the runway with hot brakes, and for some reasons we have to abort the take-off; the brakes could overheat and result in a fire. Therefore, it's important to depart with cool brakes. I also confirm that the aircraft is configured correctly and the correct runway is loaded into the flight computer (FMS). When I have verified this information, I read the checklist aloud.

When it is our turn to depart, the tower controller says, "Acme #4762, line up and wait, runway 25 right." I repeat the instructions to the controller. The captain then verbally and visually confirms that we are entering the correct runway. As we taxi onto the runway I turn on all the exterior aircraft lights. The captain steers the plane onto the runway centerline and we wait for our release. If it is my turn to fly, the captain says, "Your controls." I take the controls and respond, "My controls." I then become the pilot flying (PF) and the captain becomes the pilot monitoring (PM).

After the preceding aircraft has safely departed, the tower controller will say, "Acme #4762, cleared for takeoff runway 25 right." The pilot monitoring (PM) now responds to all radio calls and repeats the takeoff clearance. I advance the thrust levers and say, "Check thrust." The pilot monitoring verifies that the automatic takeoff thrust control system (ATTCS) engages, and then responds, "Thrust checked." I use my feet to steer the airplane straight down the runway. At 80 knots the pilot monitoring (PM) says, "80 knots." I respond by saying, "checked." We make this call to confirm that both pilots are alert, prior to entering the next critical phase of flight. If the PM fails to make the required callout at 80 knots, I question the PM. If the PM fails to respond, I assume the PM is unresponsive and I must abort the takeoff and stop on the runway.

Assuming the pilot monitoring makes the required callout at 80 knots, the next call is "V1." When the PM says V1, this call indicates that we no longer have sufficient runway distance remaining to safely stop the aircraft if an engine fails. If we lose an engine after V1, we have to takeoff. Almost immediately following the V1 call, the PM says, "rotate." I pull the yoke slowly toward my chest until the aircraft lifts off the ground and we begin flying. Now we are having fun!

After liftoff, the PM says, "Positive rate, gear up." I respond, "Gear up" and the PM retracts the landing gear. Upon reaching 1,000', the pilot flying says,

"Climb sequence after take-off checklist." The PM then raises the flaps, confirms the landing gear has retracted, and the auxiliary power unit is turned off.

During our climb, the tower controller directs us to contact the departure controller. The departure controller assigns a higher altitude, if able, and clears us to climb via our assigned departure procedure, or provides a heading to fly. The departure procedure is simply a pathway in the sky that we follow using waypoints. Most commercial aircraft are able to select from a variety of departure procedures, without having to manually enter each waypoint into the flight management system (FMS). For example, leaving LAX on the CASTA 7 Departure, we first fly to the DLREY waypoint. We then proceed to the ENNEY waypoint and remain at or below 5,000', and so on. On some departures, our speed is limited to 230 knots. We are never allowed to fly faster than 250 knots below 10,000 feet. Once above 10,000' we can fly as fast as we like, unless ATC directs us to fly slower.

If you notice that the aircraft stops climbing soon after departure, it is usually because ATC has restricted our altitude until another aircraft has passed above.

Climbing through 10,000', the pilot flying says, "10,000," and the pilot monitoring selects the "sterile switch" to the off position. In the cabin you will hear a "ding." This sound alerts the flight attendants that they may communicate with the flight deck. Below 10,000' the pilots maintain a sterile flight deck, meaning we do not speak unless the communication is related to the flight.

As we pass through 18,000', we set our altimeter to 29.92". Every pilot flying above 18,000' sets his or her altimeter to 29.92", regardless of the barometric pressure at ground level. Above 18,000' we also turn off most of the exterior aircraft lights. When we are within 1,000' of our final cruising altitude, the PF says, "1,000 feet." The last 1,000' is considered a critical phase of flight so both pilots discontinue any non-essential communication. It's important that the aircraft levels properly and acquires our cruising speed. At level flight we verify our remaining fuel, then we relax.

Chapter Nine

CRUISE FLIGHT

While flying at our cruising altitude we turn off the seat belt sign if the ride is smooth. Sometimes we completely forget to turn off the seat belt sign. Often, we don't realize our mistake until a flight attendant calls. In fact, just yesterday the flight attendant called about one hour into the flight to remind us to turn off the seat belt sign. My apologies. The seat belt sign is not mentioned on any checklist so it is often overlooked.

When I turn off the seat belt sign, I am required to make an announcement and remind you to keep your seat belt fastened, while in your seat. I think there are way too many passenger announcements. I hear some pilots making long-winded announcements while providing the winds and weather at our destination. I don't think you care about the wind in Dallas. I suspect you want to watch your movie or sleep without being disturbed by never ending announcements. Therefore, I speak softly and only make brief announcements, when required.

Depending on the duration of the flight, the captain and I eat, complain, or just stare out the window during cruise flight. As mentioned earlier, the pilot monitoring responds to all radio calls. More importantly, the PM mentally flies the airplane. The pilot flying is physically flying the airplane. Well, that's not actually true. The autopilot is probably flying the airplane. I usually engage the autopilot just above 10,000 on our departure climb. Therefore, as the pilot flying I am not always flying, I am monitoring the autopilot.

About one hour prior to landing, I begin reviewing the arrival and approach procedures at our destination airport. I also review taxi charts and highlight important radio frequencies. I also request the latest ATIS (automated terminal information system) report at the destination airport to learn the latest weather conditions and runways in use.

Prior to landing, another WANT briefing is required. As a reminder, W-A-N-T is an acronym for (weather, airport, notams, and threats). I prefer to conduct my WANT briefing during cruise flight, before we begin our descent. By the way, an arrival procedure leads us to an airport and an approach procedure leads us to a specific runway.

In addition to the weather and arrival procedure, I also brief the frequency I will use to navigate to the runway, and I discuss the missed approach procedure I will fly if we are unable to land. I also discuss the length of the runway. If the landing runway is short (less than 8,000'), I might deploy thrust reversers after touchdown to help slow the plane. By briefing various aspects of the arrival and approach, each pilot knows what to expect. That way, if I later forget something, the other pilot will question, or simply remind me. Also, by flying and acting in a consistent manner, a deviation from the norm should become apparent to at least one of the pilots. This is why air travel has become so safe during the past several decades. Pilots have been trained to utilize crew resource management. There is no longer a mindset that the captain is always right and should never be questioned. I tried this in my marriage and it didn't work either. Just kidding!

Each pilot is encouraged to question the other if something does not look, or feel right. Authoritarianism in the flight deck is dangerous. It may be beneficial in a dictatorship, but is ineffective in the flight deck. The captain and first officer work as a team and we consider ourselves equals. Well, I consider myself equal to the captain, but he or she might not feel the same about me. Of course the captain has final authority for the flight, but the first officer can assume command if appropriate.

If we are lucky, the flight management system (FMS) alerts us to our arrival gate while we are still in cruise flight. Sometimes we do not know where we will be parking until after we have landed. This is because there are so many moving pieces in aviation. The plane occupying our gate might be delayed with a mechanical issue, so flight operations has to scramble to locate another gate for us. Then, flight operations must staff the new gate with agents and rampers.

Early in my flying career I learned an important lesson. Here it is, "Be patient." At this point in my life I know that if I ever fall into a raging river, it is best to "go with the flow." If I try to swim upstream—against the current, I will get nowhere, feel exhausted, and end up downstream anyway. So be patient and go with the flow. If you miss your connecting flight you will survive. All the worry you have experienced during your lifetime got you exactly where you are right now. So why worry? Be grateful you are wealthy and healthy enough to travel by plane. When I feel frustrated and impatient I take a deep breath and remember the burn victim, a multiple amputee I saw in Las Vegas in the 1990s, when I was feeling depressed after losing $300 at the blackjack table. When I saw the badly burned amputee, it put my life in perspective. I have no problems. In life there will always be more money and other flights. Life is better when we are patient and enjoying the ride.

Chapter Ten

ARRIVAL PROCEDURE

Just like a departure procedure, an arrival procedure is a fixed route in the sky, comprised of waypoints. Think of waypoints as invisible traffic signs in the sky. Waypoints exist on aviation charts, in flight computers, and in our imagination. They don't actually exist in the sky.

Without waypoints and arrival procedures, pilots would be left to approach airports from every direction, speed, and altitude. This would create chaos, and danger would ensue. Therefore, pilots utilize waypoints to safely navigate, descend, and decelerate as we approach airports. Also, air traffic control (ATC) is able to maintain spacing between aircraft when each plane is flying at the same speed.

Large airports generally have a variety of arrival procedures, depending upon the direction of travel. When I fly from LAX to Seattle, I approach Seattle from the south. Therefore, I am usually assigned to fly the HAWKZ 5 arrival, provided the winds are favorable.

In the flight management system (FMS) I can select the HAWKS 5 arrival. Once I have selected the arrival and the pilot monitoring has confirmed the selection, the arrival waypoints are visually depicted on my multi-function display screen. If the autopilot is engaged, the airplane (should) descend and slow according to the restrictions on the arrival procedure. However, just like your home or office computer, flight computers sometimes ignore pilot commands and require a reboot. Just recently, I experienced two separate "flight computer glitches." The passengers were unaware, but ATC knew because the plane deviated from its path. One deviation occurred during our departure from Los Angeles and a second deviation occurred on our arrival into Denver.

My job as a pilot is to not only fly the airplane, but to also manage the technology. When the flight management system (FMS) and autopilot do not operate as intended, I can disconnect the autopilot and hand fly the airplane. You as a passenger will never know. I know some of you are probably feeling a little freaked out because I just mentioned that airplane computers sometimes misbehave. However, I am telling you about a day in the life of an airline pilot, and this is what happens. Don't worry! Having lots of technology in the airplane is a good thing, even if it occasionally goes awry.

By the way, I usually keep the autopilot engaged until I am 1,500' above the runway, prior to landing. You might be thinking that I am a lazy pilot. However, keep in mind that I already know how to fly airplanes. Therefore, I let the airplane do the heavy lifting. Before I became an airline pilot I never flew a plane with an auto-pilot, so I have paid my dues. If you had an auto-pilot, you would use it too! When you were a kid your parents might have made you cut the lawn using a push mower. Then one day your family bought a gas-powered mower. I bet after you got your hands on a gas-powered lawn mower you never again used your old push mower, right? It is no different when flying. Why work hard when I can work smart?

During some arrivals, ATC gets busy and leaves us high on the approach. When this happens, we have to "dive" to the airport. Meaning, we have to descend 4,000' per minute, or more. I don't like diving to the airport because I believe it's disconcerting for passengers. I like to fly so the passengers are unaware we have begun our descent. If you're on a plane and you feel yourself pointing downward at a steep angle, it's probably because the controller left the pilots too high. Remember, it's never the pilots' fault!

It is rare that I am unable to comply with a speed or altitude restriction. However, planes are similar to lawn darts. We can either descend, or we can slow, but it's difficult to do both simultaneously. To help slow the airplane, we are able to extend speed brakes. Pilots refer to speed brakes as "boards." There is a lever in the flight deck which raises a panel on the upper surface of each wing. Each panel is about the size of one Pergo floor board. The raised panels create drag and help us slow and descend simultaneously. When you hear the airplane rumble a bit during the descent, it is probably because we have deployed the speed brakes. If you look out the window you might see the raised panels. I can also extend the flaps and lower the landing gear to slow and descend faster. I must be flying slower than 250 knots before lowering the landing gear and slower than 220 knots before extending the first "notch" of flaps.

Sometimes I fly into airports without published arrival procedures. In these cases, the controller might say, "Acme #4762, proceed direct to Danger Junction Airport, descend and maintain 15,000'." When we receive ATC instructions like this, it usually means the pilots are on our own and we have to figure out the appropriate speeds and altitudes as we approach the airport. Danger Junction Airport (not its real name) may not even have an operating control tower or operating runway lights when we arrive, because the tower controller turned off the lights and went home at 10:00 p.m. Yes, I am serious. Actually, the pilots can turn on runway lights by clicking the radio frequency button several times. It seems that I only fly into Danger Junction Airports at night, in stormy weather, after the control tower has closed.

When approaching LAX, we generally fly the same arrivals procedures, so we know what to expect. Actually, I often fly over my home in Ventura County, California, when approaching LAX from the north.

After passing my home we fly over Malibu, and then turn toward downtown Los Angeles before navigating onto the final approach course.

Chapter Eleven

APPROACH

As I get closer to the arrival airport, I use our onboard navigation equipment to align with the assigned runway. Even if the weather is clear and mild, I prefer to fly the approach as if I am in the clouds and unable to see the airport. This strategy prevents me from landing on the wrong runway. You don't believe this actually happens? At San Francisco International Airport, an airline pilot nearly landed on the taxiway, adjacent to the runway, just a few months ago. Also, remember when Harrison Ford actually landed on the taxiway at the John Wayne Airport in Orange County?

Have you ever driven in an unfamiliar neighborhood and mistakenly turned the wrong way onto a one-way street? I bet you have. I have. Humans make mistakes. Pilots are still mostly human. Would you get on a plane if both pilots were robots? I bet you wouldn't. I definitely wouldn't. I accept that occasional mistakes are made. Most of the time these mistakes won't hurt us.

After flying at 37,000', it sometimes feels odd to be flying close to the ground as we approach the airport. We often fly over downtown Los Angeles at only 2,200'. What a view! At this altitude I can see the traffic backed up on the 405 freeway.

As we turn onto the final approach at LAX, ATC might say, "Acme #4762, turn right 220 degrees to intercept the localizer, maintain 2,000' until established, cleared runway 24 right approach." The controller's instructions enable us to intercept the invisible path which leads to the runway. My job as the pilot flying is to intercept an invisible beam and follow it to planet earth, preferably to a runway. With modern technology we often don't follow a beam of light (known as a localizer), because the airplane has sufficient technology to create our own path to the runway.

Despite modern technology, most of the approaches I fly utilize an instrument landing system (ILS). Even in good visibility I tune in the localizer frequency to navigate to the runway. About five miles from the runway, we cross a waypoint known as the final approach fix (FAF). I always cross the final approach fix at a specific altitude. I know the required altitude because I briefed the altitude before I began my descent and the altitude is depicted on my approach chart. When the airplane arrives at the final approach fix, if I did everything correctly and the auto-pilot is working properly, the airplane will descend at an angle of 3 degrees toward the runway. It's almost as if the airplane is following a string which extends from the end of the runway to a fixed point in space. Or, think of a "zip line" suspended from a tall tree on one end and a shorter tree on the other end. If you travel on a zip line you will move across the earth and descend simultaneously. An airplane maneuvers to the runway via a similar trajectory.

By the time I have arrived at the final approach fix, the aircraft should be fully configured. Meaning, I have extended the flaps to the desired landing configuration, the landing gear is extended, and I have slowed to my landing speed. At the final approach fix the pilot monitoring contacts the tower controller. The controller usually responds by saying that we are cleared to land. When cleared to land, the pilot monitoring turns on the center landing light, as a reminder to both pilots that we have been cleared to land.

The pilot flying (PF) commands the pilot monitoring (PM) to extend the flaps, lower the landing gear, input various altitudes, and make changes to the flight management system when the airplane is below 18,000'. Below 18,000', the pilot flying is solely responsible for flying the aircraft. The PM makes all radio calls and executes the commands of the PF. For example, when I am the pilot flying I might say to the pilot monitoring, "Flaps 1." The PM verifies that the aircraft is within the allowable flap extension speed and extend the flaps. Soon thereafter, I command "Flaps 2." Prior to reaching the final approach fix I command, "Gear down, flaps 3." The captain (pilot monitoring) will press the attendant call button and the passengers will hear a "ding" in the cabin. The pilot monitoring then moves the landing gear lever to the down position and extends the flaps to position 3. If you hear a "ding" before landing and wonder why that is, it is because of company policy. Apparently, if passengers do not hear a "ding" before we extend the landing gear, some passengers freak out when they hear the gear being lowered, because it makes a thud noise. Soon thereafter, I say "Flaps 5, before landing checklist." The captain extends the flaps to the fifth (5th) position and reads the before landing checklist. The most important part of this checklist is, "landing gear down."

Chapter Twelve

LANDING

My goal is to always land on the runway centerline, and touch down so smoothly that passengers are surprised when they realize we have landed. This doesn't always happen. When it doesn't, I usually blame mother nature. The winds are always pushing us around and sometimes a headwind changes to a tailwind just above the runway. All pilots are embarrassed by bad landings, but we all have bad landings sometimes. Even Kobe Bryant missed a basket every so often!

When I was a brand new airline pilot I once landed so hard in Atlanta that I expected a personal injury attorney to meet our plane at the gate. The flight attendants did not speak to me during the remainder of the trip and the captain was probably trying to understand how I had been hired. I was hired because there is a pilot shortage. I likely cried myself to sleep that night. I am a hard-worker and consider myself to be an accomplished person, so I feel terrible when I have a bad landing. Fortunately, I rarely have bad landings anymore.

Landing a 74,000 lb. tube in windy conditions is an art. It takes practice. Pilots practice landings in a flight simulator before flying the actual airplane, but a flight simulator is not a perfect representation of the actual airplane when it comes to landing. The first time an airline pilot ever lands a large commercial aircraft is when passengers are onboard. That's just how it is. Sadly, the only thing most passengers will remember about any flight is the landing, especially if the landing is hard. By the way, when the passengers exit the plane and say, "Great landing," it makes us feel wonderful! I can never hear that enough, so thank you!

As I am approaching the runway I often have to fly "sideways" if there is a cross-wind. When the wind is blowing from my left to my right, I point the nose of the plane into the wind, to avoid being blown off course. I steer into the wind just enough to keep the runway centerline between my legs, so to speak. Then, just before touch down, I press the opposing rudder pedal to align the aircraft with the centerline, while keeping the ailerons pointed into the wind. I am "cross controlled" when the ailerons are pointed in one direction and the rudder is pointed in the opposite direction. If pilots did not cross-control the plane prior to landing, the wind would blow the plane off-course and we might land in the grass, adjacent to the runway. That would be the end of my flying career, rightly so.

It is easy to land in good visibility and calm winds. However, if the airport is surrounded by thunder storms or a thick layer of clouds blankets the airport, things are different. If you cannot see outside, the pilots cannot see outside. I always say that any pilot can fly in good visibility. Real pilots can fly without seeing outside.

You might be interested to know that a great majority of aspiring private pilots never complete flight training. Those who do earn their private pilot certificate will never become certified to fly in the clouds. To fly in the clouds means a pilot must earn an instrument rating. Next to becoming an airline pilot, the most difficult flight training for me was becoming an instrument rated pilot. I earned my instrument rating in 1998. I still remember the first time I found myself in an airplane, flying alone in the clouds. I was scared. My heart was racing and I wondered what I had gotten myself into. I like to think I am very brave and mostly fearless, because before becoming a pilot I had served in the 3/75th Army Ranger Battalion in Fort Benning, Georgia, and parachuted 40 times from a variety of aircraft. However, flying a tiny Cessna in the clouds by myself for the first time was much scarier than jumping out of an airplane for the first time. Now I fly in the clouds so often I don't give it a second thought.

Chapter Thirteen

TAXIING TO THE GATE

After touchdown, I gently lower the nose of the airplane as we roll down the runway. The auto-brakes engage or I can manually apply the brakes. If you feel the plane decelerate suddenly after touchdown, it's because we are attempting to exit the runway quickly because the tower controller asked us to do so, or the pilots are in a hurry to get to the gate because we have to pee. Sometimes I utilize the thrust reversers to help slow the plane.

Thrust reversers allow airflow to escape from the side of the engine cowling, instead of the rear of the engine. I only use thrust reversers if we are landing on a short runway, perhaps 8,000' or shorter. In Denver, some runways are 16,000' in length. You could land the space shuttle on a 16,000' runway! If you ever land in Burbank, be assured that thrust reversers will be deployed. Burbank is notorious for their short runways. Santa Barbara also has a short runway, but if you run out of runway in Santa Barbara you will roll onto the grass at the end of the runway. In Burbank you might hit a wall, or a gas station.

Once the plane decelerates to 80 knots, the captain takes the controls if he or she was the pilot monitoring. Remember, the steering wheel is located on the captain's side. I could steer the plane into the gate using the rudder pedals. However, policy dictates that the captain must steer the plane once we are safely on the ground. Also, all captains are control freaks.

When the captain assumes control of the airplane, I resume radio communication duties. I first speak with the tower controller, then the ground controller. The tower controller will usually tell us to taxi to a particular location. At LAX and other airports, we land on the outboard runways, and must cross inboard runways to get to our parking gate. The outboard runway is simply the outermost runway. Runways are numbered based on their magnetic heading. For example, runway 25 at LAX is aligned with a magnetic heading of 251 degrees. A heading of 270 degrees is due west. In Los Angeles, the wind is usually blowing off the Pacific Ocean from the west, so we land to the west.

After exiting the runway, the captain calls for the "After Landing Sequence." I respond by turning off the landing lights, turning on the taxi light, retracting the flaps, and resetting the aircraft trim tab. The trim tab allows the airplane to fly without excessive input from the pilots.

Once clear of the runway, I contact ground control and provide our location and gate assignment. The ground controller provides taxi instructions. When the plane is moving, the taxi light is on. Day or night, I turn off the taxi light every time we stop so other aircraft and vehicles know we have stopped.

We usually need ground personnel (rampers) to guide us into the gate. Ground personnel wear a variety of hats. Sometimes they load bags. Sometimes they push the airplane away from the gate. Sometimes they guide planes into the gate.

As we taxi to the gate I often shut down one of the engines, to save fuel. Once we have stopped at the gate, I turn off the aircraft transponder so our plane is no longer illuminated on radar. The captain sets the parking brake and rampers install wheel chocks so the plane will not roll. Rampers also plug a power cord into the airplane. Once power has been established, the captain shuts down the operating engine. If there is no power cord available at the gate, we start the auxiliary power unit (APU), and then shut down the engines. Once both engines are shut down and the wheels have been "chocked," the captain turns off the seatbelt sign. Yes, there is always one person who disregards the seatbelt sign. We know who you are.

Once the engines are no longer operating, a gate agent drives the jet bridge to the airplane. When the jet bridge is positioned against the main cabin door, the agent knocks on the door and the flight attendant looks out a tiny window and gives a "thumbs up." Only then will the gate agent open the airplane door. Yes, I stop getting paid once the door opens. Ouch!

When both engines have been shut down, ground personnel begin unloading bags. Luggage that was checked at the gate will be unloaded first and brought to the jet bridge, so wait for gate-checked luggage there. Please make a line on one side of the jet bridge so other passengers can make their way to the terminal. All other checked luggage will be delivered to baggage claim.

When you see me in the airport please keep in mind that I don't know where baggage claim or anything else is located. I may have never been to the particular airport before that day. I am probably just in the airport getting some exercise or looking for a bathroom. If you have a question it's better to ask a gate agent. I just fly the plane. I don't work at the airport so I don't know where anything is. I get stopped all the time and I'm always asked the same questions. Where is this or where is that? Just look up and follow the signs!

As passengers disembark, both pilots perform a shutdown checklist. I then exit via the jet bridge and visually inspect the plane to ensure we did not strike a bird and there are no noticeable mechanical issues. If I have additional legs to fly that day, I return to the airplane and repeat the entire process. I often work 12 hour days.

Chapter Fourteen

OVERNIGHT STAYS

If I am done flying for the day, I return to the aircraft after the exterior inspection and remove my luggage. Then, the captain or I will telephone our hotel and request a shuttle van. My airline has arrangements with hotels in every city where we stay overnight. Once the flight crew arrives at the hotel, we usually go our separate ways and do not see each other again until the hotel van returns us to the airport the following day.

As I write these words, I am in a nice hotel in Vancouver, Canada. Sadly, the Vancouver hotel has no microwave or fridge in the room, and no free breakfast is offered in the morning. I landed in Vancouver at 1:00 p.m. and depart tomorrow at 2:00 p.m., for a return flight to Los Angeles, then I fly to Colorado for another overnight stay. Other than working out at a nearby gym and eating at the Denny's next door, I have not left my room. I washed my gym clothes in the shower and hung them in the bathroom so I can repack them tomorrow and they will be dry and odor free. When I arrived in Canada I smuggled several sandwiches and yogurts past Canadian customs. I heated a can of soup in the lobby microwave and helped myself to three cookies in the hotel lounge.

The only person I have spoken with since arriving at the hotel is the Denny's waitress. The hotel is located next to a freeway in an industrial area, so a relaxing walk is out of the question. This is the life of an airline pilot. It is a life of isolation, unhealthy food, and smuggled sandwiches. I cannot even call my wife as my telephone service provider charges roaming fees in Canada and I am notoriously thrifty, so I communicate via email when outside the United States.

If it is my second night in a hotel, I iron my clean uniform so it is ready to wear the following day.

If I have time to explore my surroundings I survey the area on foot. I like to walk at least 5 miles daily. In Austin or San Antonio, I can walk for hours along the river. In Boise, Idaho and Eugene, Oregon, the hotel provides bicycles to flight crews at no charge. My favorite cities usually have trails along rivers or great downtowns to explore. I enjoy staying overnight in San Diego because the crew hotel is located downtown, plus my favorite restaurant is there, The Old Spaghetti Factory (OSF). Whenever I overnight in a city with an Old Spaghetti Factory, I eat there.

This is a typical day in the life of an airline pilot.

CONCLUSION

I first considered becoming an airline pilot after I read a book by Richard Bach when I was 31 years old. I did not actually become an airline pilot until I had reached age 49. It took years of study and training to become an airline pilot. During my initial pilot training, I worked three jobs to pay for flight lessons and airplane rental. When I was not working, or flying, I studied aeronautics, navigation, meteorology, and FAA rules. Between 1998 and 2001, I spent approximately $35,000 during that time. After I had acquired 300 flight hours I was able to become a flight instructor. As a flight instructor I was able to accrue flight hours and get paid. That was a relief.

During the summer of 2001, I submitted an application to become an airline pilot. Soon thereafter, the airline industry suffered terribly. You probably remember where you were on September 11, 2001, when airplanes were used as weapons to attack the United States. Following 9/11, passengers became afraid to fly, several airlines went bankrupt, and thousands of pilots were furloughed or fired. Those were dark times in aviation.

Following the 9/11 terrorist attacks, I postponed my dream of becoming an airline pilot. In fact, I rarely flew during the following 13 years.

When I reached age 48, I re-committed to becoming an airline pilot. In my free time I began intensive training and spent thousands of dollars to relearn what I had forgotten. Then, when I was ready, I applied to become an airline pilot and was hired.

I received no scholarships, no loans, and no grants. However, I got off cheap, in my opinion, because several of my classmates in my initial airline ground school training told me that they had acquired $125,000 in flight training debt. That is a lot of money, especially when considering that the starting-pay when I was hired by a regional airline in 2015 was only $24 per flight hour. Do the math.

Starting pilot pay is often lower than what a city bus driver earns. However, I would rather fly a jet than drive a bus, so it's a faulty comparison. My hourly pay has increased significantly during the past two years, and will continue to increase if I choose to become a captain or pursue employment with a better paying airline. For now, I am enjoying life just fine. I work the first half of each month, and I am free the remainder of the month. When not working, I travel at no cost in the United States and pay very little when travelling in Europe, or elsewhere. I will receive lifetime flight benefits if I remain employed with my current airline until I reach age 58. Not a bad deal. Life has never been better!

FINAL THOUGHTS

Have you ever thought about becoming an airline pilot? If yes, read my book, "HOW TO BECOME AN AIRLINE PILOT—Achieve Your Dream Without Going Broke."

I truly believe that each of us is capable of greatness. Our thoughts, beliefs, and actions determine our results in life. If you believe the world is dangerous, unfair, and corrupt, you will likely encounter danger, injustice, and corruption. If you believe the universe is abundant, joyful, and all things are possible, you will likely experience abundance, joy, and fulfillment.

If you desire a higher income and more passion in your life, read my first book, "A BETTER LIFE—Goal Setting, Visualization, & The Law of Attraction."

During my life I have learned that I am able to create any life I desire. I am the actor, writer, and director of my life. If I don't like the scene I am in, I can write a new scene for my life. I can become a doctor, a politician, a pilot, or a circus clown. If you commit to a goal or desire, and you take inspired action, you will eventually arrive at your destination, wherever it might be. Whatever I can do, you can do too!

Turn off television news and stop reading the newspaper. The media collects the worst news from around the world and serves it up morning, noon, and night, as if nothing else is happening. If bad news is in your head, you will be focused on bad news, and what you focus on expands. Trust me on this, instead of watching television news, read uplifting books and listen to inspirational podcasts for a month and see for yourself how much your attitude and life improves.

I appreciate you taking the time to read this book. Please leave a positive review if you enjoyed my book, because your positive review means a lot to me. Say hi when you see me in the airport!

SUGGESTIONS

Some of My Favorite Authors & Speakers

Dr. Wayne Dyer

Jack Canfield

Esther Hicks

Louise Hay

Napoleon Hill

Drew Bycoskie

Marc Allen

Les Brown

Deepak Chopra

Bob Proctor

Earl Nightingale

Richard Bach

Joe Vitale

Claude Bristol

Damon Carr

Neville Goddard

Podcasts I Enjoy

The Joe Rogan Experience

Inspire Nation with Michael Sandler

The Sean Croxton Sessions

Unleash Your Passion & Step into Greatness with
Drew Bycoskie

Terry Jaymes Alive

The James Altucher Show

The Art of Charm

The School of Greatness with Lewis Howes

Theater of the Mind with Kelly Howell

Big Whig Nation with Darrin Bentley

11:11 Talk Radio

Addicted2Success

Adam Carolla Show

Duncan Trussell Family Hour

The Rich Roll Podcast

The 5 A.M. Miracle with Jeff Sanders

Author2Author

Marc Allen's Podcast

Favorite Song on My iPod

Hazy Days by Gabe Lopez

Favorite YouTube Channels

YouAreCreators

Your Youniverse

ACKNOWLEDGEMENTS

I want to thank the air traffic controllers, ground personnel, gate agents, mechanics, crew support, caterers, fuelers, baggage handlers, and all the other hard-working people who make airline travel possible. It truly is a team effort. Thank you!

I highly recommend Sheppard Air for your pilot testing and study preparation needs.

Visit their website at Sheppardair.com

ABOUT THE AUTHOR

ROBERT LAWRENCE is an airline pilot, sailor, adventurer, and an author of three books. He served in the US Army 3/75th Ranger Regiment from 1985 – 86, and is a graduate of the University of Washington in Seattle. He currently lives in Southern California with his wife and two rescue cats.